It was Gran's birthday, so
she had come to stay.
The children gave Gran a present.
'Happy birthday,' they said.
'Thank you,' said Gran.

Dad and Mum gave Gran a present.
'It's a funny shape!' said Gran.
'I can't think what it can be.'
The children laughed.
'We can,' said Kipper.

Gran was pleased with the present.
It was a Chinese vase.
'I hope you like it,' said Mum.
'It's beautiful,' said Gran. 'Thank you.'
'Put it in a safe place,' said Dad.

Gran had a surprise for everyone.
She had a box of fireworks.
She wanted a firework party.
'But I thought fireworks were
dangerous,' said Biff.

‘Fireworks **are** dangerous,’ said Gran, ‘so children mustn’t play with them,’

Mum and Gran got the fireworks ready.

They were very careful.

The children stayed out of the way.

Nadim and Anneena came to the party.

Everyone was excited.

Gran let off a big firework.

'Oooh!' said everyone.

'What a beautiful firework!' said Chip.

Dogs don't like fireworks, so Floppy stayed inside the house.

Suddenly, a firework made a loud bang.

'I don't like this,' thought Floppy, so he hid under a little table.

It was time to have tea.
Mum had a surprise for Gran.
She had a birthday cake with
lots of candles.
'Happy birthday, Gran,' said everyone.

Biff went into the front room to
get her camera.
She saw Gran's vase on the floor.
The vase was broken.
'Oh no!' said Biff.

The children went to Biff's room.
Biff showed them the broken vase.
'Gran will be upset,' said Chip, 'and
so will Mum and Dad.'
'I hope we can mend it,' said Biff.

Suddenly, the key began to glow.
The magic took the children into
a new adventure.
'Oh no!' said Biff. 'I wanted to put
the vase back downstairs!'

The magic took the children back in time.
It took them to China long ago.
Nadim knew where they were.
'We are in the Forbidden City,' he said.
'Why is it called that?' asked Chip.

'The Emperor lives here,' said Nadim.
'He lives here with his family.
Other people are not allowed to come here.
That is why it is called the
Forbidden City.'

There was a fierce dog in the
Forbidden City.
It didn't like Floppy.
The fierce dog growled and barked, but
Floppy didn't want to fight.

'Stop it!' shouted Chip.

Some women ran up and grabbed the dogs.

The children were worried.

'Oh help!' said Chip.

The women took the children and Floppy to the Emperor.

'What are you doing in the Forbidden City?' he shouted.

'People are not allowed in here.'

The Emperor called his soldiers.
'Put them in prison!' he shouted.
'That will teach them to come to
the Forbidden City.'
'I think we've upset him,' said Biff.

The Emperor had two children.
They were twins and they looked
exactly the same.
The twins spoke to the Emperor.
One of them pointed to the children.

The twins wanted to play with Kipper.
'I will put you in prison
tomorrow,' said the Emperor.
'Today you can play with the twins,'
'Hooray,' said the twins.

The twins had never played with
other children.
They didn't know how to play football.
One of the twins kicked Nadim.
'Ow!' said Nadim. 'That was my leg.'

Suddenly, the ball rolled away and
fell down a grating.
'Oh no!' said the twins.
'Now the ball is lost.'
Both the twins began to cry.

Biff and Chip pulled up the grating.
Nadim could see some steps.
He began to go down them.
'Hurry up,' said Biff. 'We don't want the
Emperor to put us in prison.'

Nadim went into a big cellar.
It was full of cobwebs and dust.
Nadim called the others.
'Look at these giant vases,' he said.
'They look like Gran's vase.'

Some people came into the cellar.
They were the Emperor's servants.
They didn't like the Emperor.
They had barrels of gunpowder, because
they wanted to blow up the palace.

The children were frightened.
They hid inside the vases.
The people didn't see them.
'We'll come back and blow up the palace tonight,' said a man.

The children ran to the Emperor.
They told him about the gunpowder under the palace.
'Some people want to blow up the palace tonight,' they said.

That night, the people came back.
The Emperor's soldiers were waiting.
The Emperor was pleased with the children.
'I won't put you in prison now,'
he said.

The Emperor had a big firework party.
There were lots and lots of fireworks.
They lit up the sky.
Everyone gasped when the fireworks went off.

Biff thought of Gran.
'I wish she was here,' she thought.
'Gran would love all these fireworks.
She'd love this adventure.'

The Emperor wanted to give the children
a present.
Biff had a good idea.
She asked for one of the big vases.
Suddenly, the magic key began to glow.

The magic took the children home.
It took the giant vase, too.
But now the vase was quite small.
'It looks exactly the same as Gran's
vase,' said Chip.

The children looked at the vases.
'Oh no!' said Biff.
'They aren't quite the same after all.
The new vase has Chinese writing on it.
Do you think Gran will notice?'